Whalers, Witches ...

Julie Irigaray

Published by Nine Pens

2021

www.ninepens.co.uk

ISBN: 978-1-8384321-0-2

For Titou Chou,
my first reader and (sometimes reluctant) proofreader

WHALERS

*"The whale fishery was first brought into notice of the southern
nations of Europe, in the fifteenth century,
by the same Biscayans and Basques,
who led the way to the fishery of Newfoundland."*
– Thomas Jefferson

Tales of the Woodcock

A picture of me holding a woodcock
my father had freshly shot
takes pride of place in our living room.
What a peculiar thing to let a three-year-old
child pose with a dead bird, and such a majestic
one. But I'm not repelled. I am familiar with

the woodcock's umber and burnt sienna
plumage – I even know her Latin name is
Scolopax Rusticola, that her belly resembles
bandages. I have learned to find the pin feathers,
these delicate stripped tears used
by artists as brushes for miniatures.

I spread her wing as one unfolds a moth, trying
not to touch the powder which allows it flight.
I'm not thinking about why her head is dangling:
I just love to caress her coal skullcap. I grasp

the woodcock tightly – my father's most precious
treasure. I don't realise yet that he will neglect
his family to track her down every weekend.
I don't resent her being our rival.

*

A snapshot of the mind: I'm no more than twelve
and my mother cooks woodcocks in boiling
duck fat to preserve them. She offers to prepare me
one for breakfast: I accept but feel embarrassed
as I know she is going to tell her friends
and all the family how good a girl from
the south west I am, eating woodcocks at 9 am:
Such a strong child, a hunter's daughter.

Now I feel guilty when I devour the woodcocks
my father shoots. I love the crack of the beak
when I open it to catch the tongue, breaking the skull
to suck the brain, the succulent taste of what I enucleate.
Then I reflect on this pair of obsidian eyes, always glassy
– the most impenetrable I've ever seen. So I make a small
sacrifice by not asking my father to bring me others,
hoping my opposition is of principle, not a rejection of him.

The Argentinian Rugby Women

Defeat is certain.
But the Argentinian rugby women
put their minds
to being defeated with honour.

The terraces are filled only with relatives,
the match broadcast on a channel no one watches –
but the Argentinian mothers stand up and yell,
wave the national flag.

They've followed their daughters
to the other side of the world
knowing they wouldn't get past the first round.

The Argentinian players display
el Sol de Mayo on their scrum caps
– their opponents tackle them without pity,
crushing them into the sludge.

The Argentinian mothers hold up:
they've dragged their husbands along,
the same men who'd refused to allow their daughters
to practise such a degrading sport.

The Argentinian mothers too
had disapproved at first.
Now they scream from the stand.

My Cricket Kids

I scan the pitch   teeming with Englishmen
wearing flannels   and helmets near the wickets

their aristocratic poise   is quaint for my expat's eyes
their China cup   skin let their blue blood appear

this is a gentleman's game   a settler's sport

or just a lazier form of baseball   both noble and debased

white-collared and starched   they emerge from
a Forster novel   or Downton Abbey

I scrutinise them with   a sardonic smile

until I realise my children   might play cricket one day

not hurling   like their father
nor pelota   like me

they will belong   to a third culture

one which will escape me   like cricket's rules

Krieg

Despite his wooden leg, my great-grandfather always
volunteered to climb up trees and pluck cherries or chestnuts.
He was the most agile of the family, as light as a sparrow.
During the second war, he was the one hiding legs

of ham in the forest by hanging them on the highest
trees so the Germans wouldn't confiscate them.
My great-grandfather was the only one in the village
who received the newspaper every day. He paid for

the subscription with his veteran disability pension.
When the gangrene spread and his leg was cut off
for the second time, my great-grandfather begged
the surgeon not to amputate it too high.

He was a farmer and no woman would want to
marry an invalid. I found his file in the military
archives. The army officer wrote after his amputation:
Leg cut 2/3 high. Can't stand the equipment.

Imaginary pain of the amputee. After the Great War,
my great-grandfather inherited the family farm
at the top of a steep hill: a barren plot of land,
a Basque Wuthering Heights nobody wanted,

let alone someone with a missing leg. The region
was occupied during the second war. One summer,
my great-grandfather and his son moved their cattle
to higher pastures for the transhumance. They reached

a point where the Germans blocked the road.
As his son was trying to negotiate their passage,
the middle-aged officer pointed at his leg and uttered:
Krieg? My great-grandfather didn't speak a word of

German, and the officer didn't speak a word of French,
so he repeated several times: *Krieg? Krieg?* The officer's
face lit up. He gestured towards the wooden leg, patted
his own chest: *Krieg! Krieg! Krieg* – a magic word

my great-grandfather deciphered in the German's eyes
and translated as: *yes I was there too thirty years ago*
I was buried alive they dug me up but my friends are still
eating cornflower roots I lost my job my fiancée too –

My great-grandfather hesitated, then finally nodded.
The officer barked orders at the soldiers, who let
my great-grandfather and his son pass with their cattle
to let them graze in peace.

Their Common Language

When my great-grandparents // wanted to communicate // without being understood // by their five children // who could speak French and Basque // they switched to Spanish // moved six thousand miles away // twenty years earlier // back to Buenos Aires // My great-grandmother had to follow // her homesick parents // back to France // she lost a country // and her freedom // My great-grandfather left // when he was drafted // for the Great War // he lost a country // and a leg // What were they saying to each other // in Spanish? // Did they resurrect a life // that was never meant to be?

The Basque Whaler

I've always wanted to drown: these six months away
hunting whales off Iceland and Newfoundland are killing me.

I've always wanted to drown:

it should be easy, I can't swim

and she could wipe us out

in one second.

The movement of her tail,

her mermaid singing exercises,

the V-shaped blow as a landmark

————————>> – I take no pleasure in harpooning

this creature of chaos and harmony.

I've always wanted to drown:

when the others chop her up

I stay in the quarters to avoid the stench of blubber.

When will I see the bay of San Sebastián again?

I am homesick, seasick, sick of

the taste of salt and vomit.

The ocean is my talisman but

I've always wanted to
drown.

Predation

Grass snakes are so graceful and harmless
with their black-and-cream choker
that the French call them necklace snakes.
They used to swim on the surface of the stream
near my window to catch minnows.

I know a sweet way to kill them: leave some bread
soaked with milk on the floor. They take pleasure
in sipping it. The crumbs swell and they suffocate.

My father fashioned a special tool to butcher them:
a metal blade attached to a wooden stick.
He took pride in tracking snakes down,
an atavism from his Basque ancestors who hunted
whales up to Iceland and Newfoundland.

Once he had forced the snake to come out of hiding,
my father moved it to firm ground, harpooned it.
His weapon wasn't sharp enough to cut it in one blow,

so the grass snake copied the twists
of its fellow creatures squashed by pitiless
Madonnas in Renaissance paintings.
Pieces of the snake were then thrown
over the garden wall like bleeding javelins.

WITCHES

"And in particular to show that the situation of the place is partly
the cause that there are so many Wizards,
it should be known that it is a mountainous country,
at the edge of three Kingdoms: France, Navarre, Spain.
The mixture of three languages, French, Basque and Spanish [...]
all these diversities make it wonderfully convenient for Satan
to hold Sabbaths in this place"

– Pierre de Lancre, the judge who conducted the 1609 Basque
witch-hunt.

The Via Appia Catacombs

Back to the womb –
miles of beehives,
Daedalus' alveoli
in the underworld
sealed with mortar.

Putrefied pigments,
depictions of Ichtys,
Christ or anchors,
the Alpha and Omega
of the resurrection kit.

Renate is your name,
yet this is your birth
to eternal pain. Poor
servant, you trusted Saint
Petronilla to protect you.

This is a religion for slaves,
martyrs and moisture,
and you are just a wrathful
Minotaur condemned to wander
in this subterranean maze.

Hecate's Cauldron

An alloy of seven metals,
the tone of a Tibetan singing bowl
reaching a celestial tone –

I use stones, the earth's bones,
no matter if they're rough or polished,
they are my jewels and my tools.

Fierce Hecate, I add tiger and falcon
eyes to my Gundestrup cauldron
to balance your energies.

Open your mouth: there is a geode
stuck in your throat, strata of inhibitions
that absorb you like a cancer of abnegation.

A sunstone to dispel depression,
a calcite for your lack of creativity,
a celestite to cure your inner child.

Himalayan salt is doomed to dissolve,
a sodalite is a small supernova,
a moss agate is mottled like blue cheese,

rock crystals are serrated teeth reflecting
a broken smile and a mutilated smoky
quartz is a man damaged by a shell.

Zugarramurdi

A rumble of guttural sounds –
their language is the oldest of the continent.
The inquisitor ogles these women:
he dreams of their tongues,
how they form foamy rollers
to hiss sensual spells
like those crashing over the shore
on the Bay of Biscay.

He's bewitched by their trilled r, their chirped z,
the way they click their k and g,
their gaping glottis when they utter the letter h.

He imagines these sorginak
grunting in grottos,
their hexes echoing on the walls.
He craves their words:
they conjure something within him,
something he's scared of.
He lusts after this language
which gave its name to their Sabbath

Blank Tongue

It is very easy
           to forget a language –
one day you're a sponge absorbing
           everything around,
the next a colander.
           A language quickly gets rusty
and turns into a nail carrying

           the tetanus of the tongue.

I lost my Spanish during the territorial
           expansion of my English.
I thought my vocabulary
           was stored at the back
of my brain, but my memory
           has buried it like a tractor
planting new seeds in a wasteland.
           What an unfruitful harvest.

It is really easy
           to forget a language,
especially a third or fourth one.
           I erased my Italian
verbs and daily-life sentences
           like chalk words written
on a blackboard as soon
           as I left the country.

It is so easy
           to forget a language
that you can even forget

your mother tongue.
My French is mixed with
    overseas swear words,
I pronounce false friends with
    the diction of a drunkard.

Magdalenian

An alignment of flints in an artificial showcase.
You gaze at the nicks, but can't feel how raw they are,
nor hold these briolette tools, gemstones from the past.
I know the plain sensation of polished pebbles in my palm,
the bang of two stones crashing in a blast of meteors.

I carved this Venus in the tundra covered with
reindeer fur to fight against the everlasting winter.
I chose mammoth ivory for this enigmatic lady.
I used to sculpt figurines, scratch rough notches
on antlers, carve spirals on tusks and ebony bones.

These are fragments of my life that you admire
behind the glass, little girl, profaning my privacy:
my broken jaw and my child's open fontanelles pass
under your scrutiny. You hunt for fingerprints on our
potteries to unearth a bond between us, the missing

element connecting the ape to yourself. You decree
archaeological excavations in your garden to dig out
arrow heads. If I brought you to the cave of the mutilated
hands, we'd paint negative stencils or elks on the walls.
This way you would find this mark of mankind in me.

Basajaun

Spirit of the Pyrenees, your name both evokes
God and the Devil. People call you *Wild Lord*
or *Lord of the Forest*, but you are:

1. **a tireless god** working seventy hours
   a week and never taking holidays.
   You use it as an excuse to take refuge
   in caves and forests every weekend.

2. **an invincible giant** who boasts about owning
   a plot of land where only you and wild boars venture.
   Once, in a ravine, a rock rolled down over your foot
   and burst it like a ripe fruit falling from a tree,
   but you managed to drag yourself back to your car.

3. **a wild man,** relentless in his relationships.
   After years roaming up and down the woods,
   your English setters are crippled with arthritis.
   When they become useless, you sell them
   to less demanding masters.

4. **an ogre** terrorising us with his fits of anger,
   a bully who can't stand frustration and revels
   in belittling us for being mere mortals.

You are both benevolent and dangerous
for those around you. You've never belonged
to us: these mountains have always haunted you,
and you keep on hunting them, Father.

GAUCHOS

"The Argentine gauchos were brutes… they didn't know how to read or write, and even less who they were fighting for. If we still remember them, it's because educated people, who were nothing like them, wrote about them."

– Jorge Luis Borges

The Wandering Gaucho

*"Three conditions must be fulfilled to be considered authentically Basque:
having a Basque surname, speaking Basque, and having
an American uncle."* – Pierre Lhande

I'm boarding for Buenos Aires
– many Basques become rich there.

I could become a pelota player in Florida
or a shepherd in California

but I've always felt like a southerner.
My ancestors were whale killers and ocean tamers,

I have nothing to lose but my youth.
I'll be a Che Guevaresque gaucho

galloping in the pampa, smoking tobacco
until my lungs burn.

I'll return with a cruel smile and gold ingots
attached to my belt. They won't believe it!

I'll marry the prettiest girl in the village
and they'll call me, with awe, *the American uncle*!

Amerikanoa

My godfather owned several hotels in Buenos Aires
but he returned to the Basque Country every year
to fish with my father, his favourite nephew.

When my sister and I married, he sent each of us a purse
filled with gold Mexican pesos. I used it to pay for
the children's college fees when my husband lost his job.

My godfather was single so he spoiled us. We didn't know
it at the time, but he'd disowned an illegitimate daughter
in Argentina. My godfather was a thug with Hemingway

looks and a cigarette glued to his mouth. I remember
the brightness of his shoes, their heady smell and smooth
tanning, the superior leather of gaucho-kept cows.

He carried a dagger with him *just in case*.
Every time I wanted to see his silver facón,
he made me sit on his knees to brush its chiselled sheath.

We never knew the details, but he'd killed a man –
we liked to imagine a heroic act: he'd stepped in
to stop a fight and had to defend himself.

When he was fishing, the children from our village
approached him with reverence, as if he were
a Basajaun who caught kids in his dragnet.

They followed him to our house,
whispering his nickname behind his back:
Amerikanoa! – the American.

During the war, when Papa was deported to eastern
Europe, my godfather chartered a boat full of goods.
We don't know how he managed to get it past

the Atlantic Wall and moor it in Bordeaux's harbour,
if he bribed someone to dispatch its contents
down south and avoid German soldiers –

we know he sent pairs of leather shoes
for all the village children,
patches of hope from the pampas.

Elegy for a Still-Alive Granny

Ravel was born in Ciboure, the village of your boarding school, Granny. From there, you used to walk back home to Cambo with your classmates, a seven-hour hike through the Pyrenees, passing St Jean-de-Luz's harbour and Bayonne's barracks while carrying backpacks, your steps following the military rhythm of his *Boléro*. As a child, Granny, you wore the traditional Basque costume during ferias: a white scarf covering your scalp, a red and black wool skirt with petticoats, espadrilles laced up around the ankles. You arched your back like a stretching cat, waiting for the txistu's drill to jump. Txistu was also your dead son's nickname as he whistled like this flute. In your youth, you used to go to village parties to dance the fandango with Spanish partners who crossed the border to seduce you, a model wearing evening gowns meant for baronesses in Biarritz balls. You now dance a dance in three- four time, your anticlockwise memory takes over the rest,   one step after another as the rhythm accelerates. Granny, you've always been triumphant when dancing, your heart beat is a metronome that never got disrupted despite the hardships,   so I want you to dance a paso doble with me one last time and we'll shout *¡Olé!* at the crowd in the arena of life before the disc scratches and the orchestra's cacophony fades into nothingness

Six War Letters

Main de Massiges, 26th September 1915

We live in perforated burrows – the landscape's wrinkles.
The trees are stakes gutting the ground.
Above us, meteored bullets whistle,
digging furrows on our foreheads.

Champagne, 9th January 1916

I've sculpted a bucket out of a shell and chiselled:
"Made in Champagne, 1916 vintage."
We'll drink in it once the Kaiser kicks the bucket.

Verdun, 27th May 1916

Men are inflammable torches: they want to be heroes
without grasping that war, at best, scorches.
Women give birth, men only give the death blow.

Chemin des Dames, 15th April 1917

Tomorrow I'll be a man: for my twenty-first birthday,
I'll be offered a battle on a plate(au) called "The Ladies' Path".
I imagine you, a Monet model crossing
this expressionist painting of pus and mud.

Chemin des Dames, 4th May 1917

Artillery shots are the earth's heartbeats.
This morning, its pulse and mine got erratic
so I held your rosary and told my beads,
mechanically. All these years I believed

I'd forgotten my prayers the way I'd forgotten God.

Chemin des Dames, 20th May 1917

Will you still love me when I'll become a cubist collage?
When pieces of my face will be glued together?
We call these men gueules cassées – broken faces.
Better for you to end up a widow.

First Phone

Children as young as you
shouldn't have phones,
your mother believed.
Rather than admitting
it was to cope,
you argued you would
get in touch with her
during school breaks
and made her promise
to send messages.

How is your tummy ache?

You never confessed
it ached
because you locked yourself
in the toilets
while a crowd outside
took part
in a papier mâché-throwing competition
with you
as a target.

You received
daily dozens
of tissue sculptures
catapulted
over your bunker.

The meds didn't make any effect.

At that stage they usually started
kicking the door
and you didn't want them
to discover you had a phone
because their insults
would have followed you
home during dinners
in front of the TV
with your family to your deathbed –

So before opening the toilet door
you ended the conversation with:

I must go now,
my friends are waiting for me.
Love

Haunted by Houses

I.

I search on Google Maps
for my childhood home:

the new owners have built an extension,
reshaped it like a Greek cross

to make it reach
its full potential –

A crucifixion of the heart
to see these impostors intruding into my past,

stealing my apricots and storing
their memories in the attic.

My mother was pregnant with me
when the first stone was laid.

We were both born together
but the house was my mother.

The roof was a womb,
the walls a placenta.

This house gave birth to three children,
yet I was the first one.

II.

In my dreams I return as if I'd never left,
as if nothing had been distorted:

the kitchen where I'd eaten woodcocks for breakfast,
the ox blood asphalt, the iron gate forged by my grandfather –

I'm a prowler. The rooms are never vacant.
I cross the wall separating the house

from the stud farm. I discover
a whole new world out of reach

and I'm cursed to search for it again.
A part of me went missing aged twelve.

How do you mourn a house?
How do you bury a childhood?

Etxe

For my partner's first visit to his village, my father brings us to the highest peak of the Pyrenees. My partner asks why the word *etxe* appears everywhere, from road signs to restaurants, town halls to hotels. My father explains it means 'house', and that the house is very important for the Basques.

My father doesn't mention a Basque would rather immolate himself and his family than lose his house. Gabriel Aresti had his people in mind when he wrote "My Father's House." My father doesn't admit losing his house would be a mutilation.

My father tells us the *etxe* is so important here his neighbours know him by the name of his house. My father forgets to add he regularly threatens to disinherit me of his every time I stand up to him.

My father explains that the eldest child used to inherit the family house so the other siblings had to emigrate to Argentina to earn a living. What he doesn't say is many of them refused to buy land in America because it would have meant bidding farewell to their Basque house.

Many Basque surnames have *etxe* as their root, like *Etxegaray.* My father deciphers our own: *Iri* = the city, *garay* = above, and at last I understand this is all about place – my surname, this visit, my angst and anger at never feeling at home in any country –

My father concludes: *it is very Basque, to leave and return.*

Notes

"**Zugarramurdi**" is a Spanish village located in the Basque Country infamous for its 1610 witch hunt. In this poem, I use the Basque word for witches, *sorginak*. The last line refers to the fact that the Spanish word for Sabbath, *aquelarre*, comes from the Basque *akelarre*, literally "the billy goat's field".

A "**Basajaun**" is a Basque mythological figure living in the woods and mountains. Described as a hairy giant, he can be either benevolent or dangerous for humans.

Acknowledgements

Thanks are due to the editors of the following journals and anthologies where versions of these poems first appeared: *Ambit, Atelier of Healing: Poetry About Trauma and Recovery, Banshee, The Best New British and Irish Poets 2018 Anthology* (Eyewear Publishing), *Foreign Literary Journal, harana poetry, Magma, Molly Bloom, Mslexia, Southword Literary Journal, Stand, The White Review*.

"Tales of the Woodcock" won 3rd prize in the 2017 Winchester Writers' Festival Poetry Competition and was longlisted for the Yeovil Literary Prize 2017. "Amerikanoa" was one of the finalists of the Mslexia Poetry Competition 2020. "Krieg" was commended in the 2020 Ambit Poetry Prize. "Six War Letters" won 2nd prize in the 2018 Winchester Writers' Festival Poetry Competition. "Etxe" was shortlisted for The White Review

Poet's Prize 2019. Many thanks to Joan McGavin, David Wheatley, Karen McCarthy-Woolf, Fred D'Aguiar, Kayo Chingonyi, Ariana Reines, and Rachael Allen, the judges of these competitions, for selecting my work.

This book would have never seen the light of day without the support and trust of my editor Colin Bancroft. I am also grateful to Natalie Whittaker for her sharp editing skills.

Many thanks to all the people and members of the Voicing our Silences collective who workshopped some of these poems. My special thanks to Romalyn Ante for her keen editor's eye, and to Maia Elsner and Serge Neptune for giving me a kick when I wanted to give everything up.

My heartfelt gratitude to Alice Hiller, who healed many wounds as a fellow poet, coach, and the most generous friend.

Thanks also to my City Lit students who give me such joy, especially Wendy Allen, and to my PhD supervisor Heather Clark for her understanding.

I cannot conclude without thanking my family (who provides me with great writing material!) and my partner for his patience towards everything poetry-related.